Self-Guidance Mindful Eating and Gratitude Journal

Eat With The Seasons

CATHY FITZGIBBON

Bookhub Publishing

Athenry

Co. Galway

Ireland

www.bookhubpublishing.com

© Cathy Fitzgibbon 2022

ISBN 978-1-7399578-1-0

Cover and inside design and layout by
Declan Durcan, MW Design Print Signs LTD. www.mwdps.ie

Cover and inside illustrations by Laura Phillips

Internal Photography by
Monika Coghlan, Pepperazzi Food Styling & Photography

The Mindful Eating Model Photography by Cathy Fitzgibbon

This publication is sold with the understanding that the Publisher/Author is not engaged in rendering health, legal services or other professional services. If legal advice, health or other expert assistance is required, the services of a competent, qualified professional person should be sought.

The paper used in this book comes from the wood pulp of managed forests.
For every tree felled at least one tree is planted, thereby renewing natural resources.

All rights reserved.
No part of this publication may be copied, reproduced or transmitted in any form or by any means, without written permission of the publishers.

A CIP catalogue record for this book is available from the British Library.

Welcome!

Thank you for purchasing this Mindful Eating and Gratitude Journal.

Here you will learn about the benefits of mindful eating and determine how to develop a healthy relationship with food, using a seasonal approach.

This journal is a positive tool to help you further explore and perhaps shift your relationship with food in a mindful and healthy way, by tracking your feelings and thoughts, whilst also offering an array of seasonal mindful eating and gratitude resources.

The practical advice and practices throughout this journal will help you experience mindful eating and gratitude. I have learned these gradually over the years, having been refined through sustained research and natural awareness in terms of my personal heightened experiences with food. Most involve techniques or mental shifts that can be embraced to help positively engage the five senses of sight, hearing, touch, smell and taste, allowing you to be fully present whilst preparing, cooking, serving, dining and enjoying food.

"Adopt the
pace of nature:
her secret is patience"

Ralph Waldo Emerson

CONTENTS

Introduction 9

Mindful Eating 11
Journaling 13
How this Journal Works... 14

Spring: Self-Reflection... 17
Spring Season Food Staples 38
Spring Season Food Experiences.. 42

Summer: Discovery 47
Summer Season Food Staples 68
Summer Season Food Experiences... 72

Autumn: Understanding and Acceptance.................................. 77
Autumn Season Food Staples 98
Autumn Season Food Experiences 102

Winter: Self-Love..107
Winter Season Food Staples 130
Winter Season Food Experiences...134

You'll See Me at The Market 139
Creating a Sacred Eating Space 141
Food Staples All Year Round 142

Top Tips..145
Epilogue..147
About the Author..155

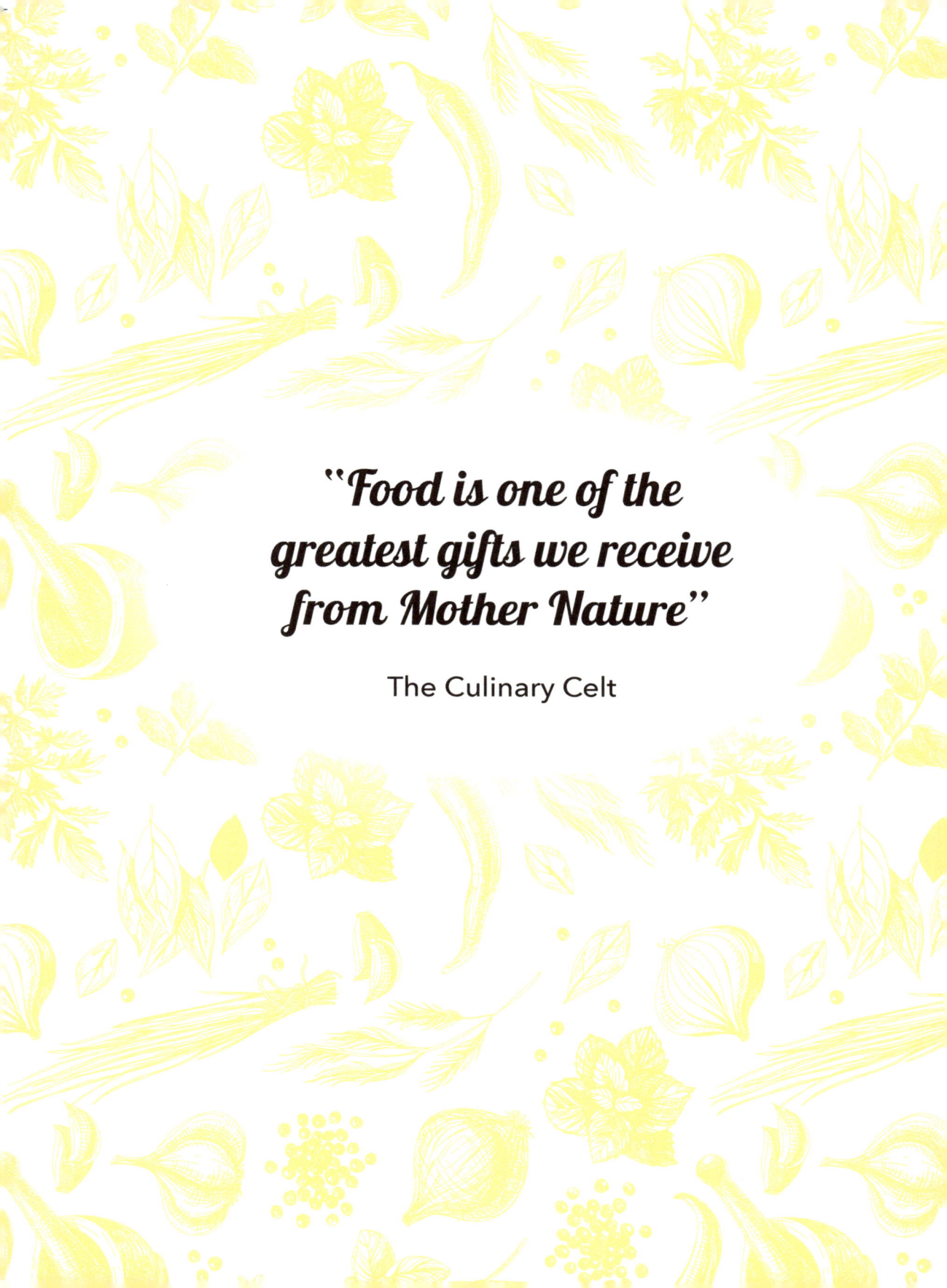

> "Food is one of the greatest gifts we receive from Mother Nature"
>
> The Culinary Celt

INTRODUCTION

We all want a sense of joy and balance when it comes to food.

Please let this be the anchor point as you begin this journal.

If you want to know what is it that interests me in food so much, then I would have to say it's the privilege of being able to co-exist with it and appreciate it for what it truly is – a nurturing wonder of the natural world.

How did this come about? Well, growing up on a farm, I witnessed first-hand, from dawn to dusk, the way food was lovingly produced using a farm to fork ethos before these words became socially on-trend! With that, my life became a roller coaster of learning processes and validation, making me further appreciate and value the source of our daily ingredients.

Marketing is my profession and making products and services appealing, by way of advertising, is my trade. Over the last three decades, I have figured out a way to combine my true love for nature and food with my profession to help educate others and amplify the voice of local businesses and food producers using a knowledgeable approach when it comes to food.

Taking the time to meet producers and uncover the value of blending traditional approaches with new age methods and technologies has enhanced my sense of harmony and overall wellbeing. Having also researched and published work on mental health relating to food, I am now ready to help you explore your own personal mindful eating journey, using my seasonal approach, methodology and tools.

This journal was written to empower you with practical and meaningful ways to self-reflect and understand your eating patterns in tune with nature and the four varied seasons of the year, enabling you to build a more positive and fruitful relationship with food.

Cathy aka The Culinary Celt x

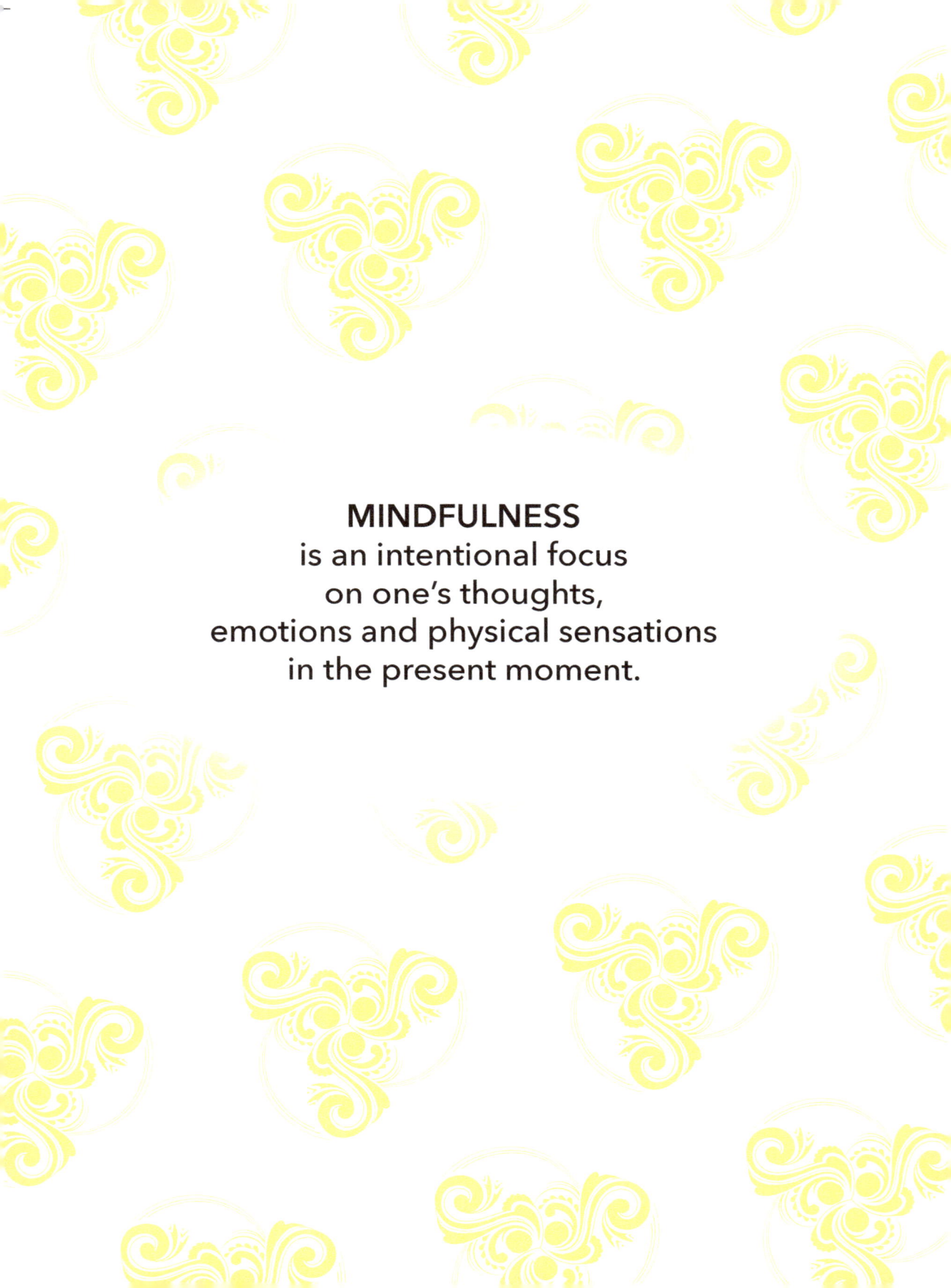

MINDFULNESS
is an intentional focus
on one's thoughts,
emotions and physical sensations
in the present moment.

MINDFUL EATING

Mindful eating originates from the vast philosophy of mindfulness, now used by many of us in our everyday lives. Eating mindfully involves the use of all our physical and emotional senses to fully immerse ourselves in the experience of enjoying our food choices. The intention is to target becoming more aware of, rather than reacting to, our situation and food choices. It encourages making choices that will be satisfying and nourishing to the body whilst also discouraging judging eating behaviours, as there are many different types of eating experiences. This type of mindfulness helps to increase gratitude for food, which in turn, can help improve our overall eating experience, as it revolves around the presence and awareness of our own unique food experiences. As we become more in tune with our eating habits, we may then take steps towards behaviour changes that will benefit both ourselves and our environment, whilst also welcoming the development of positive relationships with food.

Mindful eating is not a diet. It focuses predominantly on our 'in the moment' eating experiences, body-related sensations, and thoughts and feelings about food, with heightened awareness and without judgment. Close attention is paid to the food we choose to eat, as well as internal, external, physical and environmental cues and our responses to them. It is a practice that cultivates inward investigation to promote more enjoyable meal experiences and a better understanding of our eating environment.

Mindfulness and our Relationship with Food

Bringing mindfulness into our relationship with food can be very revealing. When we honestly look at how and why we engage in various eating patterns it is truly amazing what can be discovered.

If we struggle with food, this may be because we feel stuck in certain habits of doing the same things over and over, getting the same unwanted results which, in turn, can lead us to a lack of confidence in terms of our food choices and subsequently our nutritional intake. The difficulties can stem from lack of knowledge, personal circumstances, social status and a wide range of ingrained reactions to unrecognised triggers around food, comprising of thoughts, feelings and situational cues. The idea of mindfulness in terms of food lets us approach eating from another angle. Mindfulness can increase awareness of subliminal patterns which can influence us more than we know on a conscious level. The insight gained from mindful food practices can help create new actions that achieve alternative results.

JOURNALING
is an emotional, mental and spiritual
exercise that helps us build
'emotional muscles' to help deal with
life's uncertainties and difficulties.

JOURNALING

The practice of journaling is the act of expressing our deepest thoughts and feelings by putting words to our inner life on paper. In identifying our negative thoughts and beliefs and cultivating positive healing ones in their place, journaling can help us discover our sense of purpose and meaning in life.

Being a vehicle of emotional exploration, journaling is a way that difficult feelings can be channelled into healthy and creative outcomes. By writing down our thoughts and feelings, we are forced to slow down and pay attention to everything that is going on in life. This form of free self-expression leads to exploration and personal growth. When our feelings are expressed through written expression, we can begin to work through our problems, rather than avoiding them. Journaling can also help bring a sense of inner peace and tranquillity which has been shown to help us destress, eat healthier and boost self-confidence.

Food journaling is one of the most powerful things we can do. Identifying the foods that we eat everyday makes us more in tune and aware of what, when and why we eat, whilst at the same time helping us discover our eating patterns and habits.

Identify the 'Whys'

Why do we eat when we're not hungry? Why do we buy certain foods over others? These are all questions that food journaling can help answer. Making note of our energy levels, mood, and body satisfaction allows us to explore food choices that benefit our overall wellbeing. This type of mindful awareness and learning can help identify specific food types that don't serve us well. These realisations become powerful tools that enable us to form positive eating patterns and help support 'friendly' relationships with food.

HOW THIS JOURNAL WORKS

This journal was developed using a seasonal approach. You may start it at any time of the year during any of the four seasons, then continue it through the annual cycle. It has been designed to empower you with meaningful ways to self-reflect and understand your eating patterns throughout each of the four seasons. Containing a selection of themed inspiring quotes along with an array of helpful mindful eating and gratitude tips, with plenty of room for writing and journaling your findings, this guided journal will walk you through the seasons giving you a variety of gentle prompts and timely encouragement along the way.

Years of trawling through food markets has educated me that the most enjoyable and nutritious food can be found in simplicity of form - unique and natural in the way mother nature intended them to be. The shape, size and natural elements of food has a profound impact on aspects of taste and overall nutritional value. The illustrations showcased as season food staples are bespoke in design by Laura using a distinctive artistic style that mindfully reflects the Culinary Celt ethos, by way of striking visuals and authentic context.

As you delve into each of the sections contained within this journal my teachings focus on a four-pillar framework that I have developed called 'The Celt Mindful Eating Model'. These four common elements carried throughout each season have been designed to enable you to build a positive relationship with food by mindfully embracing and actioning on this methodology:

Consider the Food Source
Enjoy and Be Present
Love your Food
Take Notice of Your Feelings

Consider the Food Source

Do you know your local food producers? It's a personal decision, but in my opinion it's important to care where our food comes from, as this connection helps us develop a healthy relationship with food, by making us more grateful and aware of what we are eating. It is important to know more about what we eat, as getting an adequate amount of nutrients to fuel the body is crucial to our overall wellbeing. Eating locally sourced ingredients also means money stays in our communities and food does not travel as far to get to our homes. Less travel means less carbon emissions which in turn helps create a sustainable impact on the environment.

Enjoy and Be Present

If you find yourself eating in front of the television, computer, or other distractions such as mobile phones, try switching them off temporarily the next time you find yourself in this pattern. By focusing on your food, the bites you take, and your level of hunger, you may discover that you are eating emotionally. Actioning these changes to your eating patterns will give your mind time to catch up with your stomach. Eating mindfully is a skill that takes time and practice. Learn to enjoy new experiences in the here and now without self-judgement.

Love your Food

Our relationship with food is a mirror image of our relationship with life. It is important to always enjoy and appreciate food. Never feel guilty about the past. When it comes to this, I find it best to draw a line in the sand. Don't be hard on yourself based on past experiences or feel bad about what you have eaten. Alternatively, be in love with the conscious choices you make every time you eat. Feel the love and energy that you get from food, as it sustains and gives us life.

Take Notice of Your feelings

Feelings of shame and guilt are associated with emotional eating so it's important to work on the positive self-talk you experience, or this may lead to a constant cycle of emotional eating behaviour. Instead of being hard on yourself, try learning from your setbacks and reward yourself with self-care measures. It is also important to seek support and resist isolation in moments of anxiety or sadness. Even a quick phone call to a friend or family member can do wonders for our mood. Additionally, there are a variety of formal groups that can also help to offer support.

TERMS OF USE

The contents of this journal are for educational purposes and are not intended to offer personal medical advice. You should seek advice from your physician or other qualified health providers with any questions you may have regarding a medical condition. Never disregard professional medical advice or delay in seeking it because of something you may have read here. I do not recommend or endorse any specific eating styles or types of food. My ethos is more about using a practical seasonal approach when it comes to food.

Spring Season
SELF-REFLECTION

"Spring will come
and so will happiness.
Hold on. Life will get warmer"

Anita Krizzan

SPRING: SELF-REFLECTION

Welcome to Spring Season

SPRING is a season of new beginnings. By this virtue, farmers and gardeners plant their seeds. Buds begin to bloom, animals that have hibernated over the winter start to appear and the earth starts to come to life again, making it a great time to reflect and take in all the goodness that it has to offer.

When using this section of the journal, it will be important to give yourself some personal space for the sake of self-reflection, to focus on the different components of your eating patterns.

WHEN DO YOU EAT?
When do you feel like eating, think about eating, or decide to eat?

_____

WHAT DO YOU EAT?
With a diverse range of food options available, what do you choose to eat?

_____

WHERE DO YOU EAT?
Where do you physically eat?

_____

WHY DO YOU EAT?
Why do you eat at chosen times?

_____

HOW MUCH DO YOU EAT?
How do you decide on the volume of what you eat?

_____

Start asking yourself these questions. Sometimes simply posing them begins the process of awakening insight.

SEASON START POINT

Body Scan
Write down where your body is at in terms of your attitude towards food:

_____

_____

_____

_____

_____

_____

_____

This component of mindfulness meditation is a helpful way to get in touch with the body and release any pent-up emotions.

Environmental Scan
Write down where you are at in terms of being consciously connected with your natural environment:

_____

_____

_____

_____

_____

_____

_____

This natural awareness in terms of the connection with your local area as a food source brings about a harmonious sense of balance.

EMOTIONAL EATING AWARENESS

Emotional eating comprises of the countless daily stresses that can at times cause us to seek comfort or find distraction in food. Physical and emotional hunger can often be easily confused but are noticeably different in a variety of ways. Several factors, including hormonal changes, stress and a multitude of mixed hunger cues can bring about emotional eating.

Physical Hunger

- Develops gradually over time
- Can be satisfied with any food types
- No negative guilty feelings towards eating
- You stop eating once full
- Eating more mindfully
- Need for energy from food

Emotional Hunger

- Comes about suddenly / abruptly
- You desire / crave specific types of food
- Feelings of shame or guilt after eating
- You continue to eat when full
- Eating more mindlessly
- Finding comfort in food

Pay attention to how and when your hunger starts, as well as how you feel after eating. While filling up may satisfy in the moment cravings, eating because of negative emotions can often leave us feeling more upset than before. This cycle typically does not end until we address our emotional needs head-on.

Discovering ways to deal with negative emotions is the first step toward overcoming emotional eating. This is where journaling, getting regular exercise, reading a book, or finding a few minutes to relax and unwind from the day can help with shifting your mindset from reaching for food to engaging in other forms of stress relief.

A quick yoga or meditation routine may also help during these particularly emotional moments. Simple deep breathing is a meditation that you can do almost anywhere. Sit in a quiet space and focus on your breath. Experiment with a variety of activities to find what works best for you. My top three key areas to look at and consider are:

1. Eat a healthy diet
Make sure to get enough nutrients to fuel your body. As mentioned, it can be difficult at times to distinguish between physical and emotional hunger however if you eat well throughout the day, it can be easier to spot when you are eating emotionally out of sadness, boredom, or stress.

Reaching for healthy snacks, like fresh fruit or vegetables and other low-fat, low-calorie foods at these times will help to maintain healthy eating patterns. Having a fresh fruit bowl on your table and using it to make fruit salads and prepare smoothies to have ready to drink can be good options for in between mealtime snacks.

2. Take common offenders out of your kitchen
Keeping food, you crave when feeling emotional out of reach can help to break any unhealthy eating cycles, by giving you more time to think before eating. It is also important to plan food shopping, delay food shopping trips and never stock up whilst feeling hungry or upset.

3. Pay attention to portion sizes
Measuring out portions and choosing smaller plates to help with portion control are mindful eating habits worth developing. Eating a healthy balanced diet is not only about what you eat – it is equally about how much you eat and the variety of food from the different food groups[1]. These building blocks will help you get a good balance of daily nutrients, needed to fuel the body.

---

1. Fruits, Vegetables, Grains, Protein Foods and Dairy

KICK-START YOUR MINDFUL EATING LIFESTYLE

Helpful Spring Season Mindful Eating Habits

- Consider incorporating a morning gratitude meditation practice into your daily routine.

- Find new seasonal recipes and add them to your springtime meal plans. Get some inspiration from my spring season food staples in this section of the journal.

- Plan to make and enjoy at least one meal a week that's veggie based. I am not vegetarian but find this helps me consciously consume a good variety of fruit and vegetables on selected days.

- Stock up on non-perishable staples such as grains, flour, spices and pasta.

List some healthy mindful eating habits here that you would like to embrace and continue to use daily this season:

_____

_____

_____

_____

Trust

Renewal   Grow

Rebirth

Bloom   Emotional

Spring

Reflect   Happiness

Joy

Mindful   Patterns

Imagine   Balance

Barefoot

FOOD AND MOOD DIARY

Day	Time	Food/Drink Types	Emotions Before Eating	Emotions After Eating	Observations
Monday					
Tuesday					
Wednesday					
Thursday					
Friday					
Saturday					
Sunday					

In terms of food, I am grateful for: _____

_____

_____

THE CELT MINDFUL EATING MODEL

 The **C** in my *Celt Mindful Eating Model* represents - **C**onsider the Food Source

In springtime I use a helpful colour coding system when it comes to sourcing ingredients.

Spring in my mind represents green, so I tend to focus on using lots of seasonal greens such as asparagus, wild garlic, leeks, cabbage and lettuce in the dishes I prepare and enjoy this time of year.

When it comes to meat and fish, spring lamb and responsibly sourced fish types including whiting, haddock and lemon sole feature on my weekly meal plans.

This spring season what variety of foods have you eaten and where do they originate from?

What my spring dishes look like

THE CELT MINDFUL EATING MODEL

E The **E** in my *Celt Mindful Eating Model* represents - **E**njoy and Be Present

I find it rewarding to carve out time each day to develop cooking patterns that work for me in keeping with each season. Choosing to either steam, grill, bake or boil my foods depending on the ingredients in my shopping basket. I tend to steam a lot of my food in springtime, grill a lot in summer, bake a lot in autumn and boil a lot in winter. Learning new and enjoyable ways to cook can be very therapeutic and can help transform the way you think about food, introducing you to a more engaged healthy eating lifestyle.

What have you learned from both your cooking and eating patterns this season?

THE CELT MINDFUL EATING MODEL

 The **L** in my *Celt Mindful Eating Model* represents - **L**ove your Food

I wear my heart on my sleeve when it comes to food. My motto is to always move with the seasons. With this point of view, I use a two-fold approach:

1. Respect all the work that has gone into the production of it before it reaches my home and
2. Appreciate and value the ingredients by savouring them in my eating experience.

What foods have given you the most pleasure this season and why?

THE CELT MINDFUL EATING MODEL

T The **T** in my *Celt Mindful Eating Model* represents - **T**ake Notice of Your Feelings

At the start of this section, I touched on the fact that it's important to give yourself space to self-reflect and take notice of your feelings when it comes to food. Emotional eating awareness will empower you to figure out your bodies needs and wants, as these factors will continue to evolve and change.

How have you felt this season, did you encounter any difficult moments worth making note of here?

MINDFUL EATING FOOD DIARY

Place at home, restaurant, work, in the car, at desk, table, on lap, in bed	People alone, with friends, family, work colleagues	Activity reading, watching TV, listening to music, talking	Hunger Rate from 0 to 5 0 = not hungry 5 = very hungry	Food	Fruit and/or Veggies Quantity of servings	Fullness after Eating Rate from 0 to 3 1 = still hungry 2 = satisfied 3 = discomfort

Place at home, restaurant, work, in the car, at desk, table, on lap, in bed	**People** alone, with friends, family, work colleagues	**Activity** reading, watching TV, listening to music, talking	**Hunger** Rate from 0 to 5 *0 = not hungry* *5 = very hungry*	**Food**	**Fruit and/or Veggies** Quantity of servings	**Fullness after Eating** Rate from 0 to 3 *1 = still hungry* *2 = satisfied* *3 = discomfort*

SPRING SEASON FOOD STAPLES

Rhubarb
An excellent source of Vitamin K, important for bone health metabolism and formation, which may help aid the prevention of osteoporosis.

Wild Garlic
This powerful food contains both Vitamins A and C ideal for warding off bacteria and viruses without harming our gut flora.

Asparagus
Bursting with nutrients including Vitamins A, C and K, this vegetable cultivated for its spring stalks improves digestion and high blood pressure conditions.

Lamb
Rich in high-quality protein and Vitamin B12 this meat source helps promote muscle growth, maintenance and performance.

Purple Sprouting Broccoli
This nutrition superstar contains an abundant amount of valuable nutrients such as Vitamins A, K, folic acid and low carbohydrates, all of which accelerates reduced hunger and improved cognitive performance.

SPRING SEASON FOOD STAPLES

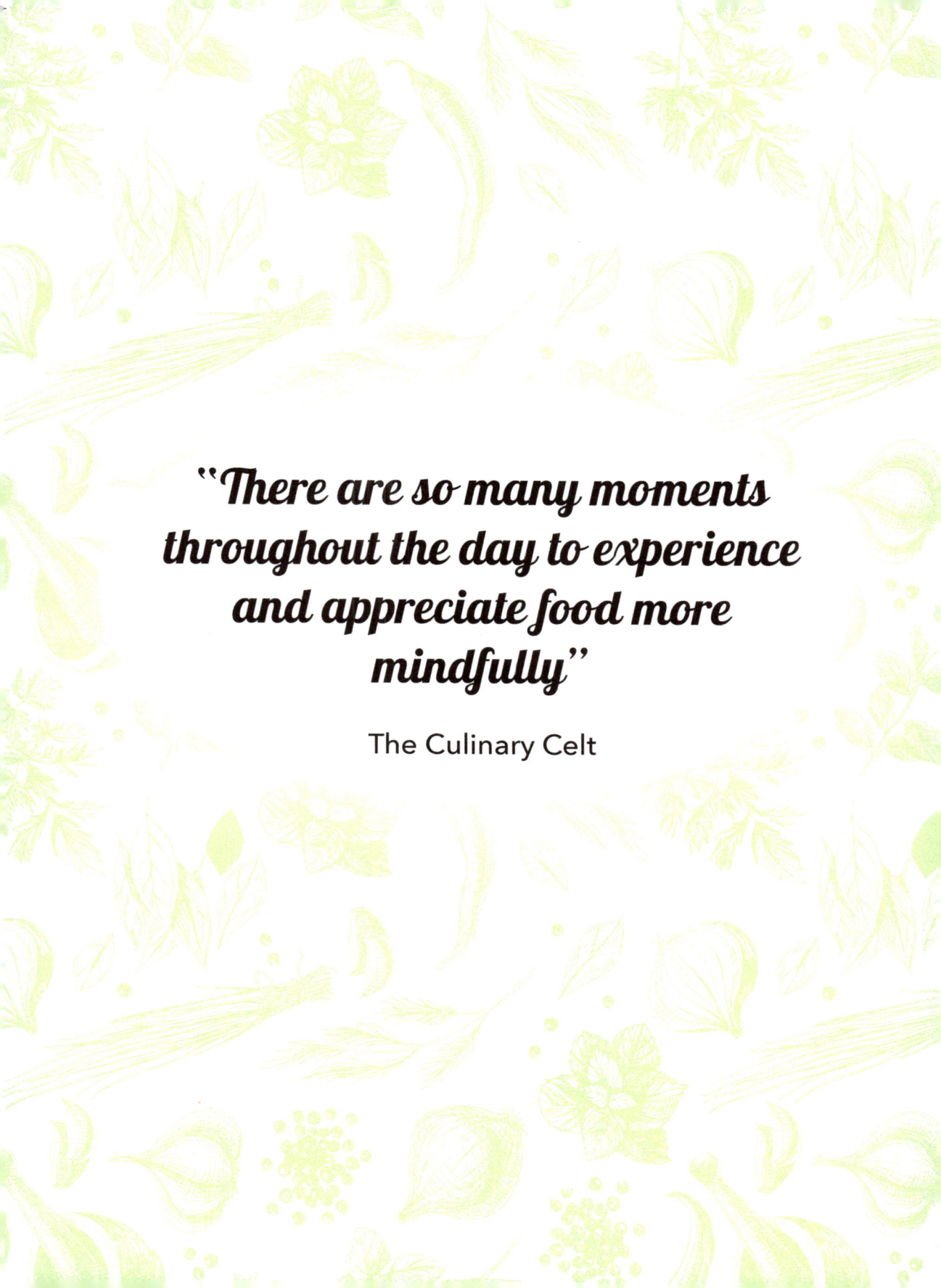

"There are so many moments throughout the day to experience and appreciate food more mindfully"

The Culinary Celt

THE SECRET TO MINDFUL EATING AND GRATITUDE ENGAGEMENT

Mindful eating is also a way to practice gratitude during mealtimes. It allows us to slow down the pace of our meals, pay attention to how our bodies respond to food, whilst giving us time to appreciate the eating process.

Benefits to Practicing Gratitude:

- Gratitude brings us happiness by boosting our feelings of optimism as well as other positive emotions.

- Gratitude is good for our bodies and can help strengthen our immune system, lower our blood pressure, and reduce symptoms of illness. It also encourages us to take better care of our health and exercise more.

- Grateful people get more sleep, spend less time trying to fall asleep, and feel more refreshed upon waking up.

If you would like to cultivate more gratitude in your life, try focusing on mealtimes. Remember a lot of unseen work happens before food appears on your plate. Many people have played different roles from tilling the fields, planting seeds, harvesting the crops to transporting the food to allow us to purchase it to eat. If you are dining with others, remember to appreciate your relationships and the time you spend together. Feel free to share your gratitude out loud with family and friends or simply pause for a few silent moments before starting and enjoying each meal.

In terms of food, I am grateful for: _____

_____

_____

_____

_____

SPRING SEASON FOOD EXPERIENCES

- Spring is a great time of year to think about planting and growing a selection of easy to maintain seasonal herbs, fruit and vegetables. It's a fascinating experience that you can do by yourself or incorporate it into a family experience.

- Plan and enjoy a spring-themed home dining experience with family and friends.

- Spring is also full of fascinating scents in the great outdoors. Take time to notice the aromas around your garden and local area and mindfully get curious with them. This type of experience can be rewarding arousing your senses on many levels.

- Get out and talk to local food producers and farmers. They will be able to offer you an array of tips and advice when it comes to seasonal food choices. It's good to know where and how ingredients are grown so you can fully appreciate all the work that goes into your meals.

SPRING – SEASON SUMMARY
Self-Reflection

What are the main nuggets that you have learned from this section?

SPRING – SEASON SUMMARY
Self-Reflection

Are you noticing any patterns in terms of your eating habits?

SPRING – SEASON SUMMARY
Self-Reflection

Summarise the efforts you have made this season in terms of your mindful eating and gratitude rituals:

~ Summer Season ~
DISCOVERY

> "I love how summer just wraps its arms around you like a warm blanket"
>
> Kellie Elmore

SUMMER: DISCOVERY

Welcome to Summer Season

SUMMER begins on the day of the summer solstice (the longest day of the year) and ends on the day of the autumn equinox. It is a season of warm, hot long days, while nights are the shortest, making it the best season to spend time enjoying the outdoors.

When using this section of the journal, it will be important for you to set your intentions and be willing to learn more about your own relationship with food and how it can influence your lifestyle choices.

WHEN DO YOU EAT?
When do you feel like eating, think about eating, or decide to eat?

_____

WHAT DO YOU EAT?
With a diverse range of food options available, what do you choose to eat?

_____

WHERE DO YOU EAT?
Where do you physically eat?

_____

WHY DO YOU EAT?
Why do you eat at chosen times?

_____

HOW MUCH DO YOU EAT?
How do you decide on the volume of what you eat?

_____

Start asking yourself these questions. Sometimes simply posing them begins the process of awakening insight.

SEASON START POINT

Body Scan
Write down where your body is at in terms of your attitude towards food:

_____

_____

_____

_____

_____

_____

_____

This component of mindfulness meditation is a helpful way to get in touch with the body and release any pent-up emotions.

Environmental Scan
Write down where you are at in terms of being consciously connected with your natural environment:

_____

_____

_____

_____

_____

_____

_____

This natural awareness in terms of the connection with your local area as a food source brings about a harmonious sense of balance.

"If you don't love it, don't eat and if you love it, savour it"

Evelyn Tribole

MINDFUL EATING: A JOURNEY OF SELF-DISCOVERY

First, we need to bring a gentle awareness to the present moment and understand that we live in the now. Then begin to visualise what the future looks likes and set intentions for what we want to achieve. Doing this using mindful eating practice involves meditations which will help us to become calm, focused and alert. We will also be better able to manage emotions, ignore distractions, control impulses and process what we are thinking and feeling, resulting in more mindful choices.

It is extremely important to identify our physical cues. Use simple, mindful activities to help the body tune in to sensations of hunger, thirst, fullness and gratification. Eliminate grazing and try not to eat two hours before each meal to build up an appetite. It is the art of mindful eating and the continuous daily rituals that will help achieve real success.

Food should make us feel good and nourish our bodies. The next step is to determine what your body wants for nourishment. If we seek food but perhaps are not truly physically hungry, we could be craving social connection, stimulation, attention, or physical exercise. Becoming aware and utilising wisdom concerning areas of nutrition and fitness will help mould a healthy body and mind.

There are no labels on foods when it comes to mindful eating – food is not 'good' or 'bad', a reward or a punishment. When eating mindfully there should be no restrictions or deprivation. When food is restricted, it tends to become central to our thinking. We can then start to obsess over it, crave it and eventually binge on it, resulting in feelings of shame and guilt that may over time create long-term negative relationships.

Permit yourself to enjoy food. Have freedom and flexibility about the foods you eat, but structure mealtimes where everyone sits together without any distractions. Eat with pleasure, savour food, celebrate the moment, allowing no place for shame or guilt. Try to choose quality over quantity.

Remember when you introduce mindful eating into your home it takes time and consistency, however the rewards will become apparent. These gradual changes become invisible habits leading to the development of a wholesome mindful eating culture.

KICK-START YOUR MINDFUL EATING LIFESTYLE

Helpful Summer Season Mindful Eating Habits

- The best way to navigate summer eating is to embrace a balanced mindset. Stop thinking about dieting options and learn more about your relationship with food.

- The warmer weather and longer brighter evenings in summer create great opportunities to stay active and enjoy the outdoors in your local area and amenities. Create a schedule that fits into your work and life commitments and mindfully incorporate it into your daily routine.

- Summer is a great time to learn something new. I have upskilled in areas such as photography, cooking techniques and lots of new learning around food waste and sustainability. Pick some topics that you would like to develop and incorporate this knowledge into your lifestyle.

- Take a 'Digital Detox'. Consider taking some time away from your screens and get out into nature more. Quality time outdoors is invaluable. It's important to allocate time to switch off from our various online sources and carve out that quality time to find gratitude in the great outdoors.

List some healthy mindful eating habits here that you would like to embrace and continue to use daily this season:

_____

_____

_____

_____

Radiant

Enjoy Flexible

Pleasure

Celebrate Reward

Summer

Habits Discover

Hydrate

Natural Taste

Wellbeing Respect

Sustainable

FOOD AND MOOD DIARY

Day	Time	Food/Drink Types	Emotions Before Eating	Emotions After Eating	Observations
Monday					
Tuesday					
Wednesday					
Thursday					
Friday					
Saturday					
Sunday					

In terms of food, I am grateful for: _____

_____

_____

THE CELT MINDFUL EATING MODEL

 The **C** in my *Celt Mindful Eating Model* represents - **C**onsider the Food Source

Colour coding comes into play for me in sourcing summer ingredients.

For me, summer represents the colour red so in this season my food choices are vibrant and focus on incorporating lots of seasonal fruit and vegetable options such as strawberries, tomatoes and beetroot into the dishes I cook and prepare.

Due to shifts in warmer weather I enjoy experimenting making different types of salads and BBQ dishes. Meats like chicken and fish like mackerel are flavoursome seasoned with fresh herbs, some of my favourites being parsley, basil, coriander and dill.

This summer season what variety of foods have you eaten and where do they originate from?

_____

_____

_____

_____

_____

_____

_____

What my summer dishes look like

THE CELT MINDFUL EATING MODEL

 The **E** in my *Celt Mindful Eating Model* represents - **E**njoy and Be Present

Being conscious of how our everyday food choices have both a macro impact on our planet and a micro impact on local areas and communities is extremely grounding and a humbling 'present in the moment' experience. Taking personal responsibility for eating sustainably is at the forefront of my day-to-day food choices. My mantra is carried through the words of Signey Sheldon *"Try to leave the earth a better place than when you arrived"*.

What have you learned from both your cooking and eating patterns this season?

_____

_____

_____

_____

_____

_____

_____

_____

THE CELT MINDFUL EATING MODEL

 The **L** in my *Celt Mindful Eating Model* represents - **L**ove your Food

One of the guiding principles that forms part of my process in terms of mindfully loving food is 'Quality over Quantity'. I take this approach in both meal planning and food shopping. Taking a small bit of time out each week to think about the dishes I will use the ingredients in, the quantities needed and the seasonal nutritional value of my overall food choices.

What foods have given you the most pleasure this season and why?

_____

_____

_____

_____

_____

_____

_____

_____

_____

THE CELT MINDFUL EATING MODEL

 The **T** in my *Celt Mindful Eating Model* represents - **T**ake Notice of Your Feelings

I find it extremely therapeutic using physical cues such as music to form part of my daily eating rituals when it comes to mealtimes. This type of preparation helps positively engage my senses, heightening my sense of awareness, allowing me to build a more fulfilled and positive relationship with food.

How have you felt this season, did you encounter any difficult moments worth making note of here?

_____

_____

_____

_____

_____

_____

_____

_____

_____

MINDFUL EATING FOOD DIARY

Place at home, restaurant, work, in the car, at desk, table, on lap, in bed	**People** alone, with friends, family, work colleagues	**Activity** reading, watching TV, listening to music, talking	**Hunger** Rate from 0 to 5 *0 = not hungry* *5 = very hungry*	**Food**	**Fruit and/or Veggies** Quantity of servings	**Fullness after Eating** Rate from 0 to 3 *1 = still hungry* *2 = satisfied* *3 = discomfort*

Place at home, restaurant, work, in the car, at desk, table, on lap, in bed	**People** alone, with friends, family, work colleagues	**Activity** reading, watching TV, listening to music, talking	**Hunger** Rate from 0 to 5 *0 = not hungry* *5 = very hungry*	**Food**	**Fruit and/or Veggies** Quantity of servings	**Fullness after Eating** Rate from 0 to 3 1 = still hungry 2 = satisfied 3 = discomfort

SUMMER SEASON FOOD STAPLES

Strawberries

Rich in Vitamin C, folic acid, potassium, fibre and antioxidants this fruit helps support heart health, lower blood pressure and guard against cancer.

Beetroot

Loaded with Vitamin B9 this powerful vegetable can be consumed regularly to benefit overall health. Betacyanin, the purple colour pigment in beetroot, can have an aiding effect on liver function.

Mackerel

This fish source contains a significant amount of Vitamin B12 and vital omega-3 fatty acids that help our body produce anti-inflammatory compounds, making it great for conditions such as eczema, asthma and arthritis.

Tomatoes

Containing Vitamins B and E this nutrient-dense superfood benefits a large range of bodily functions.
Their nutritional content aids healthy skin and may also mitigate the risk of developing diabetes.

Onions

This kitchen staple contains Vitamins A, B6, C, E and minerals such as sodium, iron, potassium and dietary fibre. Their anti-inflammatory properties help fight inflammation, reduce cholesterol levels and protect against blood clots.

SUMMER SEASON FOOD STAPLES

> *"How we feed our body is linked to how we treat the planet"*

The Culinary Celt

Eating Sustainably

With so much food now produced worldwide, making it available all year round, it can be easy to lose track of its seasonality. It is equally important to create awareness of your external environment by way of delving into and discovering how your lifestyle choices and relationship with food impact the local natural environment. Addressing these ultimately gives us a better chance to live more healthily and harmoniously within the ebb and flow of the seasonal cycles of the year.

Respecting our Food Sources

Seasonal eating varies by location and fluctuates based on weather and climate variations. Food has seasons but unfortunately, at times, in our busy day-to-day lifestyles we can become removed from this fact. Animals follow the ebb and flow of the year through their natural life cycles producing tastier and healthier meat when slaughtered in their proper season. To eat the freshest, healthiest, and most humanely raised meat available you should learn the seasons for your favourite meats.

Winter Rule
**Four Legs Good,
Two Legs Bad
with Lamb being an Exception**

Vegetables and other types of food such as fruit, pulses and grains should also be selected, grown and eaten with the different seasons in mind. At times frozen fruit and vegetables can also be a very good nutritious option to avoid food wastage. Fruit and vegetables are fresher and tastier when in season as they will have been harvested recently and grown locally.

Benefits of Eating Locally Produced Seasonal Food

- It is more nutritious and tastes superior as the time from 'place to plate' is considerably less.
- It offers an environmentally friendly solution due to its shorter journey to stores.
- It has a far better carbon footprint than foods which have been transported from other countries, thousands of miles around the world.
- It requires less preservatives and as a result tends to be fresher, being more of a farm to fork offering.

SUMMER SEASON FOOD EXPERIENCES

- Summer is an ideal time for picnics and outdoor dining experiences. The warmer weather makes it great for these types of casual dining options. Dining outdoors has the power to change our mood as it moves us away from our normal eating routine and more relaxing experiences can also help create special memories.

- Camping at festivals is very popular during the summer months. Get organised and find a festival to enjoy. Glamping options are now also a super idea at outdoor festivals so pitch up your tent and explore the food options, music and fun there!

- As different fruit comes into season during summer, learning how to make refreshing lemonades and cocktails is an enjoyable adventure. Tomatoes, cucumbers and other seasonal fruit and vegetables make a fabulous base for a wide range of cocktail recipes.

- Pickling is a great way to extend the shelf life of food using either brine or vinegar, then left to ferment for a specific period of time (varying on the recipe you use). Beyond cucumbers, other summer fruit and vegetables that work well for pickling include beets, onions, tomatoes, carrots and fennel.

SUMMER – SEASON SUMMARY
Discovery
What are the main nuggets that you have learned from this section?

SUMMER – SEASON SUMMARY
Discovery

Are you noticing any patterns in terms of your eating habits?

SUMMER – SEASON SUMMARY
Discovery

Summarise the efforts you have made this season in terms of your mindful eating and gratitude rituals:

– Autumn Season –
UNDERSTANDING & ACCEPTANCE

"*Autumn shows us how beautiful it is to let things go*"

Anon

AUTUMN: UNDERSTANDING AND ACCEPTANCE

Welcome to Autumn Season

AUTUMN is a magnificent season for fresh local produce, as it signals harvest time. It's a season of preparation, when farmers start to collect their crops and wonderful abundant varieties of fruit and vegetables. Varied shades of colour can be seen dotted around the countryside providing the opportunity to spend quality time outside connecting with nature and appreciating this joyous slow-paced season.

When using this section of the journal, it will be important for you to find flow in terms of what works for you and give yourself space and time to understand that when it comes to food 'Mindful Moments' all add up.

WHEN DO YOU EAT?
When do you feel like eating, think about eating, or decide to eat?

_____

WHAT DO YOU EAT?
With a diverse range of food options available, what do you choose to eat?

_____

WHERE DO YOU EAT?
Where do you physically eat?

_____

WHY DO YOU EAT?
Why do you eat at chosen times?

_____

HOW MUCH DO YOU EAT?
How do you decide on the volume of what you eat?

_____

Start asking yourself these questions. Sometimes simply posing them begins the process of awakening insight.

SEASON START POINT

Body Scan
Write down where your body is at in terms of your attitude towards food:

_____

_____

_____

_____

_____

_____

_____

This component of mindfulness meditation is a helpful way to get in touch with the body and release any pent-up emotions.

Environmental Scan
Write down where you are at in terms of being consciously connected with your natural environment:

_____

_____

_____

_____

_____

_____

_____

This natural awareness in terms of the connection with your local area as a food source brings about a harmonious sense of balance.

FOOD
may help ease emotions initially but
addressing the feelings behind the hunger
is important in the long term.

EATING HABITS AND BEHAVIOURS UNCOVERED

It is natural to find comfort in food. However, in my experience unless we tune into the daily practice of mindful eating how we feel can at times negatively influence what we choose to eat. Healthy eating means eating a variety of seasonal foods that give us the required nutrients needed to maintain overall health, so learning and adapting to how our food seasons and cycles work will help us make healthier and more mindful choices. This type of positive understanding enables taking charge of your appetite, giving a better feeling of calm, high energy levels and alertness from the foods consumed. Changing deep-rooted, unhealthy eating habits will ultimately help create improvements in overall health and a more positive relationship with food.

Many of us tend to use food as a coping mechanism to deal with feelings such as stress, boredom, anxiety, or even to prolong feelings of joy. While this may help in the short term, eating to soothe and ease feelings often leads to regret and guilt, and can even increase the negative feelings towards food. To be successful in terms of your own eating habits and behaviours, be aware of the role that eating plays in your life and learn how to use positive thinking and behavioural coping strategies to manage your eating mindfully. Whilst filling in the tried and tested *Take Notice of Your Feelings* section of my four-pillar 'Celt Mindful Eating Model', in this journal, your own eating patterns and habits will start to become more apparent.

Here are a few tips to help get you started:
- Keep track of your eating habits.
- Plan meals and snacks ahead of time.
- Don't skip meals.
- Drink plenty of water.
- Try to distract yourself when you experience cravings.
- Exercise instead of eating when you're bored.
- Eat in proper dining settings (kitchen table).
- Watch portion sizes.
- Allow yourself to eat a range of foods without denying yourself certain food types.
- View healthy eating as a lifestyle change.

KICK-START YOUR MINDFUL EATING LIFESTYLE

Helpful Autumn Season Mindful Eating Habits

• Being a transition season, autumn is a really good time to add more warm and nourishing foods such as soups and stews to our meals to prepare the body for the upcoming winter season.

• Food alternatives are a great way to adjust this season. I changed from having a glass of orange juice in the mornings to having a glass of apple juice instead, as apples are grown here in my local area and I can source local apple juice.
Orange juice, on the other hand, is non-native and needs to be sourced from warmer countries, so that one food change alone has helped to reduce my carbon footprint.

• Our skin being the largest organ of the body needs to be looked after and rejuvenated on a daily basis. I keep mine hydrated by drinking water and eating a rainbow of colourful fruit and vegetables (at least five portions a day) to help naturally improve it.

• Yoga is an important exercise that I incorporate into my weekday routine. I find it helps relax my body whilst also offering me a sense of gratitude and a balanced peace of mind.

List some healthy mindful eating habits here that you would like to embrace and continue to use daily this season:

_____

_____

_____

_____

Alive

Prepare   Connect

Understand

Accept   Calm

Autumn

Triggers   Harvest

Nourish

Question   Abundance

Flavour   Leaf

Gentle

FOOD AND MOOD DIARY

Day	Time	Food/Drink Types	Emotions Before Eating	Emotions After Eating	Observations
Monday					
Tuesday					
Wednesday					
Thursday					
Friday					
Saturday					
Sunday					

In terms of food, I am grateful for: _____
_____
_____

THE CELT MINDFUL EATING MODEL

 The **C** in my *Celt Mindful Eating Model* represents - **C**onsider the Food Source

I use a helpful colour coding system when it comes to sourcing ingredients.

Autumn being harvest season is a fantastic time to enjoy earthy foods such as carrots, pumpkins and honey. I view it kindly as a season of preservation and change and a chance to reconnect with nature through my food choices.

For me, this golden season comfortingly helps prepare my body for the winter season ahead by way of beef stew dishes and pumpkin soup combinations made with herbs like fresh mint or chives.

This autumn season what variety of foods have you eaten and where do they originate from?

What my autumn dishes look like

THE CELT MINDFUL EATING MODEL

 The **E** in my *Celt Mindful Eating Model* represents -
Enjoy and Be Present

The slow pace of this transition season gives us the time to accept and understand any deep-rooted unhealthy eating habits which may have formed over time. I personally use this season to embrace any mental shifts that are needed to help engage my senses. I do this by taking the time to work on my in the moment thoughts relating to sight, hearing, touch, smell and taste and offer gratitude for the fact that I have them all at my disposal to enjoy.

What have you learned from both your cooking and eating patterns this season?

THE CELT MINDFUL EATING MODEL

 The **L** in my *Celt Mindful Eating Model* represents - **L**ove your Food

For me, love in autumn season represents nourishing and comforting my body alongside understanding and accepting all that it provides.

I look to nature to help me with this and find inspiration from the varied autumnal shades that help me process and understand the fact that not everything is black and white when it comes to food. We are all different and that's what makes us unique. It's important to allow ourselves to be our own best version of ourselves.

What foods have given you the most pleasure this season and why?

THE CELT MINDFUL EATING MODEL

T The **T** in my *Celt Mindful Eating Model* represents - **T**ake Notice of Your Feelings

The sensory pleasures that we get from the taste of food can determine our food intake. With this in mind during these moments of mindfulness I tend to satisfy my tastebuds with a variety of seasonal foods to help nourish my body. This approach helps overcome any cravings I have and also keeps the need for unwanted food at bay during my day-to-day life.

How have you felt this season, did you encounter any difficult moments worth making note of here?

_____

_____

_____

_____

_____

_____

_____

_____

_____

MINDFUL EATING FOOD DIARY

Place at home, restaurant, work, in the car, at desk, table, on lap, in bed	People alone, with friends, family, work colleagues	Activity reading, watching TV, listening to music, talking	Hunger Rate from 0 to 5 0 = not hungry 5 = very hungry	Food	Fruit and/or Veggies Quantity of servings	Fullness after Eating Rate from 0 to 3 1 = still hungry 2 = satisfied 3 = discomfort

Place at home, restaurant, work, in the car, at desk, table, on lap, in bed	People alone, with friends, family, work colleagues	Activity reading, watching TV, listening to music, talking	Hunger Rate from 0 to 5 *0 = not hungry* *5 = very hungry*	Food	Fruit and/or Veggies Quantity of servings	Fullness after Eating Rate from 0 to 3 1 = still hungry 2 = satisfied 3 = discomfort

AUTUMN SEASON FOOD STAPLES

Beef

For meat eaters this provides an excellent dietary source of iron and essential vitamins such as riboflavin, niacin, Vitamins B6 and B12 which help reduce tiredness and fatigue.

Apples

A great source of Vitamin C this popular fruit also contains pectin, a fibre that helps with gut health. It's worth noting that it is best to leave the skin on when eating them because it contains more than half of the apple's fibre.

Honey

Being a rich source of phenols and antioxidant compounds this versatile and staple food promotes health in several ways. It can naturally help the body with antibacterial, wound-healing and anti-inflammatory effects.

Pumpkins

This superfood is one of the healthiest vegetables you can eat containing Vitamin C, E, iron, and folate promoting eye health and a healthy cholesterol.

Blackberries

Packed with Vitamin C and K these berries offer a wide range of health benefits including bone development, oral health and brain health.

AUTUMN SEASON FOOD STAPLES

> "Nature's seasonal bounty should be our menu of the day"
>
> The Culinary Celt

MENTAL SHIFTS TO ENGAGE THE SENSES

The word diet can hold a lot of very different meanings. Some may define it as the types of food that we eat daily while on the other spectrum others believe it to be restricting oneself to small amounts or special types of food to aid with weight loss. For me, the latter is a label which I don't choose to engage with. It should be about eating healthy daily and not about restricting ourselves from any specific types of food. Have you ever noticed that a different sequence of the word **Diet** spells **Tied**… and that it is! Restricting ourselves when it comes to food and tying into certain diets may unhinge mindful eating. Paying attention to the bite sized moment-by-moment experience of eating is a wonderful experience to help engage our senses.

TUNING INTO YOUR 5 SENSES

Sight

Being caught up in today's busy lifestyles we can at times eat without realising the beauty that goes into the food that we consume. Take the time to notice and become more aware of and connected to the ingredients on your plate.

Hearing

This involves considering your food source. So, get out daily and embrace nature! Listening to the natural source of the different produce that you consume can be very rewarding. Nature nurtures and it's a grounding experience to note that soil is an incredible material that when tilled turns into leaf, flower and fruit.

Touch

It's important to become more in-tune and aware of the ingredients that you are preparing and cooking. Pay attention to the uniqueness and textures when it comes to freshly grown fruit and vegetables, in the way they look and feel.

Smell

Ground and immerse yourself in the present moment of eating. Enjoy the fruits of your labour and notice the combination of aromas from the food that you have taken the time to cook and prepare.

Taste

Savour the taste and texture of the food you eat. Being mindful when eating is extremely important as it can help aid digestion.

AUTUMN SEASON
FOOD EXPERIENCES

- Apple pressing is an alternative way to utilise this harvest season's fruit and make delicious apple juice. Pressing equipment such as fruit presses and crushers can easily be brought online.
Alternatively, look out for local farmers markets that offer this service during autumn season.

- Foraging - the act of searching for food provided by nature can be a very rewarding experience. Blackberries, elderberries and mushrooms are good examples of berries and fungi that you can be on the lookout out for this season. Be careful when it comes to mushrooms, get familiar with the types and species so you know they are edible and safe to cook and eat.

- Whether it's a day trip or a longer breakaway a food truck dining experience is a must! Food trucks have come a long way in the last few years having become extremely innovative. The selection and variety of creative menus and the location of food trucks make them a winning combination to enjoy.

- A lot of ingredients that we buy whether it be fruit, vegetables, or other types of leftovers can end up in the bin before they've been used to their full potential. Soups, smoothies and omelettes and many other dishes are great ways to repurpose food and cut down on excessive food waste.

AUTUMN – SEASON SUMMARY
Understanding and Acceptance
What are the main nuggets that you have learned from this section?

AUTUMN – SEASON SUMMARY
Understanding and Acceptance
Are you noticing any patterns in terms of your eating habits?

AUTUMN – SEASON SUMMARY

Understanding and Acceptance

Summarise the efforts you have made this season in terms of your mindful eating and gratitude rituals:

~ Winter Season ~
SELF-LOVE

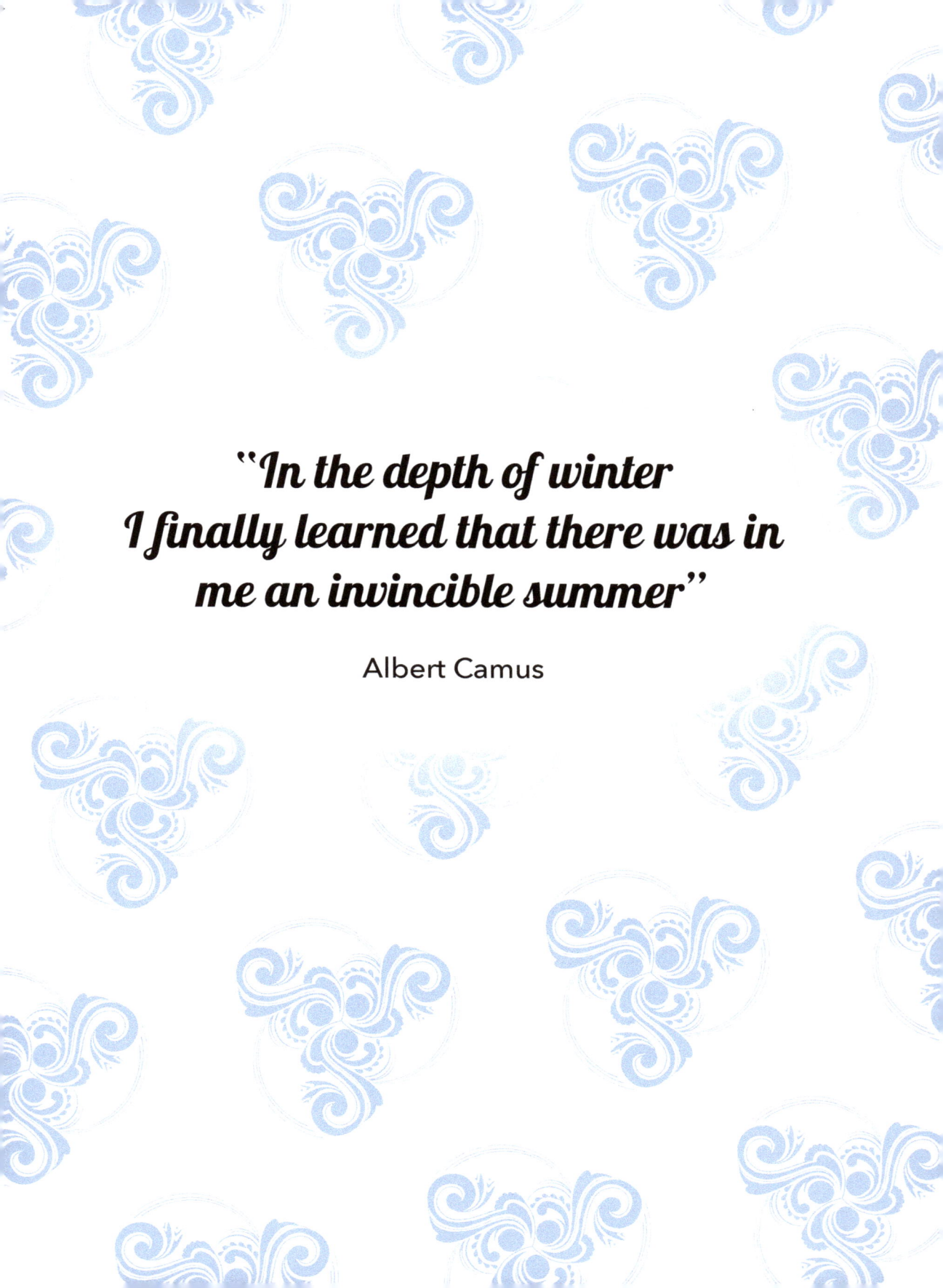

"In the depth of winter
I finally learned that there was in
me an invincible summer"

Albert Camus

WINTER: SELF-LOVE
Welcome to Winter Season

WINTER being typically the coldest season of the year is associated with a dramatic reduction in air temperatures and icy weather. This season brings with it many changes, the impact and timing of which varies according to location. The distinctive cold weather and reduced daylight hours have a huge influence on vegetation by way of limiting plant growth, causing some animals to migrate to warmer areas.

When using this section of the journal, it will be important for you to look inward and listen and respond to your body in terms of practicing self-love.

WHEN DO YOU EAT?
When do you feel like eating, think about eating, or decide to eat?

_____

WHAT DO YOU EAT?
With a diverse range of food options available, what do you choose to eat?

_____

WHERE DO YOU EAT?
Where do you physically eat?

_____

WHY DO YOU EAT?
Why do you eat at chosen times?

_____

HOW MUCH DO YOU EAT?
How do you decide on the volume of what you eat?

_____

Start asking yourself these questions. Sometimes simply posing them begins the process of awakening insight.

SEASON START POINT

Body Scan
Write down where your body is at in terms of your attitude towards food:

_____

_____

_____

_____

_____

_____

_____

This component of mindfulness meditation is a helpful way to get in touch with the body and release any pent-up emotions.

Environmental Scan
Write down where you are at in terms of being consciously connected with your natural environment:

_____

_____

_____

_____

_____

_____

_____

This natural awareness in terms of the connection with your local area as a food source brings about a harmonious sense of balance.

*"Eating well is
one of the easiest ways
to love yourself"*

Roxana Jones

SELF-LOVE: FROM A CULINARY PERSPECTIVE

There are no right or wrong ways to build self-love. It is vitally important to remember that it's an ongoing process and your inner compass is always there to guide and help you with this. Learning to live mindfully every day and embrace mindful eating and gratitude takes understanding and patience so it's important to be able to dig deep and discover what works for us all on a personal level. Past mistakes may have been signposts pointing us towards what we need to work on. It's best to view them as an opportunity to confront our overall relationship with food.

As part of cultivating a healthy mind and body, we need to participate in habits that encourage self-love. Self-love can mean a variety of different things when it comes to food, but in a nutshell, it involves feeling good about yourself. Far too often we depend on others for this type of validation. But it's crucial to look inwards and use your individual internal compass to help with this. Using my 'Celt Mindful Eating Model' framework in this journal will help with this journaling aspect.

These are a cross-section of some helpful areas to focus on:

Respect Your Body
Practice self-love and respect your body by way of exercising and eating healthy. View your body as a temple, a place to tune into and listen. This type of daily respect will help prevent negative actions and enable refraining unhealthy behaviour when it comes to food.

Stop Comparing Yourself to Others
Time spent thinking that we are less than others, because they may appear to have more and look differently decreases self-love. This type of comparison with others can often lead to feelings of depression and loneliness, so try to hold yourself up in your daily interactions.

Focus on Your Self-Talk
Find ways to counteract negative self-talk and align it with conversations that are more loving and compassionate with nature. Eating mindfully can really help with this as being in tune with food and nature is a powerful positive ripple effect that can help aid self-love.

"Suppose you are
drinking a cup of tea. When you
hold the cup, you may like to breathe in,
to bring your mind back to your body,
and you become fully present.
You must be completely awake in the present
to enjoy the tea. Only in the awareness of the
present can your hands feel the pleasant warmth
of the cup. Only in the present can you savour
the aroma, taste the sweetness, appreciate the
delicacy. If you are ruminating about the past,
or worrying about the future,
you will completely miss the
experience of enjoying
the cup of tea"

Thich Nhat Hanh

ALIGNING OUR INNER COMPASS

To assist you in this section of the journal, from a seasonal food perspective, my Culinary Compass guidance tool was designed to help identify where you are at in terms of your own self-love journey and navigate you towards the direction that you wish to be better aligned with.

This guidance tool is divided into four areas, aligned with the four cardinal points: north, south, east and west. It will help you examine yourself from different angles and perspectives and make it easier for you to work on where you would like to be better positioned.

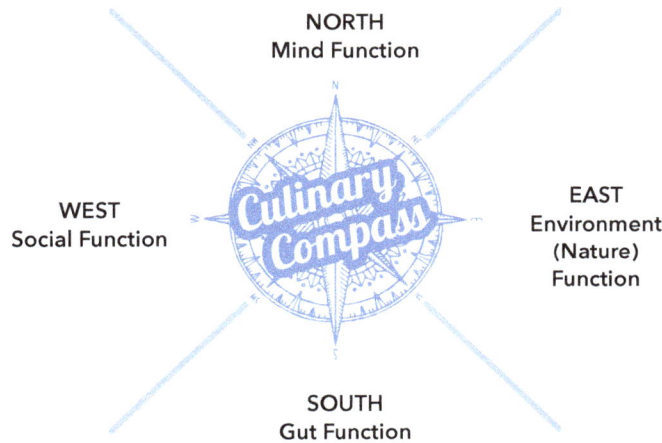

When it comes to food a routine scan of where you are at and where you would like to be in life is very important. As you journey through this section of the journal and explore each of these aspects in more detail it will help give you greater overall balance when it comes to establishing rewarding seasonal eating patterns.

Write down here the compass directions you have yet to explore and the value that exploring them would add to your daily lifestyle:

_____

_____

_____

_____

KICK-START YOUR MINDFUL EATING LIFESTYLE

Helpful Winter Season Mindful Eating Habits

• Learn how to make your own bread.
There are lots of simple recipes for bread so download one online or pick up a good cookbook and get baking! I bake small batches to enjoy them with my winter soups and stews.

• Make your own hot chocolates and read by the fire.
I find food history and culture fascinating to read about. We can learn so much from generations that have gone before us in terms of food. There's lots of knowledge out there and reading and applying the information learnt can be extremely beneficial to our everyday lives.

• Pick one aspect of the 'Mindful Eating Compass' to work on daily during the winter months to help maintain balance:
NORTH – Mind Function
SOUTH – Gut Function
EAST - Environment (Nature) Function
WEST – Social Function

• The colder weather this season can increase the temptation to eat comfort foods. I try to resist the urge by having small cups of homemade soup or a bowl of stewed fruit to address the gaps if I'm hungry between meals.

List some healthy mindful eating habits here that you would like to embrace and continue to use daily this season:

_____

_____

_____

Beautiful

Self-Love   Warmth

Peace

Direction   Forgive

Winter

Change   Kindness

Listen

Season   Believe

Positive   Brave

Nature

FOOD AND MOOD DIARY

Day	Time	Food/Drink Types	Emotions Before Eating	Emotions After Eating	Observations
Monday					
Tuesday					
Wednesday					
Thursday					
Friday					
Saturday					
Sunday					

In terms of food, I am grateful for: _____

_____

_____

THE CELT MINDFUL EATING MODEL

The **C** in my *Celt Mindful Eating Model* represents - **C**onsider the Food Source

Winter is all about comfort so I get creative in the kitchen using richer seasonal food to help guide me in my choices.

My mission in wintertime is to seek out comforting food options that help keep my inner compass aligned. Unfortunately, my local farmers market closes each year from mid-December to the start of February so it can be a difficult time to source an abundance of fresh fruit and vegetables this season. However, brussels sprouts, kale and turnips are some of my favourites and a variety of other all year-round foods help further satisfy my selection of winter mealtime dishes.

This winter season what variety of foods have you eaten and where do they originate from?

What my winter dishes look like

THE CELT MINDFUL EATING MODEL

E The **E** in my *Celt Mindful Eating Model* represents - **E**njoy and Be Present

To help develop a healthy mind and body I honour myself selflessly by enjoying my 'in the moment' mealtime experiences. This type of positive inner-self talk can help shift our mindset and validate any moment-by-moment unwanted feelings that don't serve us with a positive relationship when it comes to food.

What have you learned from both your cooking and eating patterns this season?

THE CELT MINDFUL EATING MODEL

 The **L** in my *Celt Mindful Eating Model* represents - **L**ove your Food

Winter is not my favourite season! If I'm to be completely honest the colder weather, at times, can make me slightly irritable. With this in mind I'm learning to accept how I feel and this helps alleviate a lot of the tension and stress caused by denying and rejecting it.

The key is to centre your needs and wants around 'Self-Love' this season. When it comes to food, each season offers a multitude of choices for us to appreciate.

What foods have given you the most pleasure this season and why?

THE CELT MINDFUL EATING MODEL

T The **T** in my *Celt Mindful Eating Model* represents - **T**ake Notice of Your Feelings

A healthy and balanced diet can help alleviate numerous health problems. Our bodies give us signals to tell us that something may be out of balance with our diets. Being in tune with and acting on our body signals is a form of self-enquiry that can help us to feel more fulfilled and enable us to get closer to our true selves. I find journaling and taking notice of food patterns works as it gives me the clues that I need at times to adjust the food that doesn't serve my body well.

How have you felt this season, did you encounter any difficult moments worth making note of here?

MINDFUL EATING FOOD DIARY

Place at home, restaurant, work, in the car, at desk, table, on lap, in bed	People alone, with friends, family, work colleagues	Activity reading, watching TV, listening to music, talking	Hunger Rate from 0 to 5 0 = not hungry 5 = very hungry	Food	Fruit and/or Veggies Quantity of servings	Fullness after Eating Rate from 0 to 3 1 = still hungry 2 = satisfied 3 = discomfort

Place	People	Activity	Hunger	Food	Fruit and/or Veggies	Fullness after Eating
at home, restaurant, work, in the car, at desk, table, on lap, in bed	alone, with friends, family, work colleagues	reading, watching TV, listening to music, talking	Rate from 0 to 5 0 = not hungry 5 = very hungry		Quantity of servings	Rate from 0 to 3 1 = still hungry 2 = satisfied 3 = discomfort

WINTER SEASON FOOD STAPLES

Brussels Sprouts

Rich in Vitamin K this powerful winter weather superfood is
jam-packed with high levels of nutrients
that are linked to several health benefits.
Their high fibre content supports digestive health
and can help reduce the risk of diabetes and heart disease.

Turnips

A powerhouse of nutrition this root vegetable is a great source
of fibre and Vitamin A, C and K. Traditionally used for treating
various ailments such as rheumatoid arthritis, inflammation,
and headaches they offer a multiple range of health benefits.

Venison

Grass fed on summer pastures, this meat is a great source of
B Vitamins, in particular Vitamin B12 and Vitamin B6.
Being low in fat and cholesterol means it can play a vital role in
both brain and nervous system function.

Pak Choi

This leafy green vegetable offers a variety of
Vitamins A, C, E, K and minerals as well as fibre and
antioxidants making it beneficial for the thyroid function,
heart health and bone health.

Kale

Loaded with powerful antioxidants, along with
Vitamins A, K, B6 and C, this vegetable boasts an impressive
nutritional profile, making it an ideal food source which may aid
a variety of health conditions such as bone and eye health.

WINTER SEASON FOOD STAPLES

*"Dare to discover
the magic within food"*

The Culinary Celt

NAVIGATING 'THE CULINARY COMPASS TOOL'

It is important when it comes to food to examine how we navigate our human experience. My work in food education highlights the importance of tuning into the seasons and learning how our daily food choices can help create a greater sense of harmony and balance to our lives. Going micro is key, so with this in mind 'The Culinary Compass Tool' contains four key areas:

North – Mind Function

Whether we like it or not the food we choose to eat contributes to our mood and our brain functions best when we maintain a well-balanced and nutritious diet. Eating high-quality seasonal foods with adequate amounts of vitamins, minerals and antioxidants can help nourish the brain whilst also protecting us from other types of stresses.

South – Gut Function

An increasing amount of scientific evidence highlights the important role that food plays on our gut microbiome and overall health. Keeping our gut healthy is not only important for digestive health but it also contributes to our overall physical health and mental wellbeing. The gut communicates with the brain through a series of nerves and hormones making it important for us to mindfully discover ways to fuel our gut health daily, by way of our seasonal food choices.

East - Environment Function

The way we acquire, prepare, and consume food has an immense impact on our environment and our daily food choices play a contributing factor towards global climate change. This creates the need for us to become more conscious in looking after the environment, bringing our families up in a more sustainable way.

West - Social Function

Be it direct, indirect, conscious, or subconscious, the impact of social influence refers to the eating behaviour of others and how at times these external influences help sway our own personal food intake. Even when we eat alone our food choices are influenced by social factors which stem from attitudes and habits developed through our social interactions with others. As food fulfils an array of both social and psychological needs it is equally important to take the time to explore and uncover our own eating patterns from this viewpoint.

WINTER SEASON FOOD EXPERIENCES

- Get creative in the kitchen and recreate some of your favourite takeaway dishes. Fakeaways are an ideal way to replicate them. I enjoy making homemade versions of Asian style stir fry dishes and have learnt ways to adapt them slightly to incorporate the use of seasonal winter ingredients such as pak choi, kale and brussels sprouts.

- Winter months are a great time to try out new restaurants. It's a mood boosting way to get through the season. These types of food experiences are best shared in good company and can be a positive way to connect with family and friends.

- It may be difficult to get motivated to cook during winter. Faced with shorter evenings of daylight, a slow cooker is a hassle-free way to cook a wide variety of delicious meals. Investing in one and learning how to cook using it will help see you through these colder months.

- Taking a cooking class is an opportunity to gain self-confidence and learn how to prepare several types of dishes in a shared environment.
No matter if you're cooking for one, two or meal planning for the whole family, these types of classes can help get you out of the routine of making the same meals.

WINTER – SEASON SUMMARY
Self-Love
What are the main nuggets that you have learned from this section?

WINTER – SEASON SUMMARY
Self-Love
Are you noticing any patterns in terms of your eating habits?

WINTER – SEASON SUMMARY
Self-Love
Summarise the efforts you have made this season in terms of your mindful eating and gratitude rituals:

> "In my food world, there is no fear or guilt, only joy and balance"

Ellie Krieger

YOU'LL SEE ME AT THE MARKET

For the past three decades I have been a customer of farmers markets. Trips there will open your eyes to a variety of seasonal fruits and vegetables that may never find their way to our local supermarkets. At farmers markets we can often find foods native to the area as well as gorgeous varieties of fresh local produce to enjoy.

Many of the stallholders and farmers of local markets are not only proud of the food they produce and sell but they are also eager to share helpful information, tips and recipes that can help you get the most out of your purchases. From my own personal experience, having grown up on a dairy and tillage farm, farmers are a wealth of knowledge when it comes to seasonal food.

Here's a flavour of some food markets that I've visited from around the world:

Fremantle Markets
Perth, Australia

The English Market
Cork, Ireland

Farmers Market
Siem Reap Cambodia

Mercado San Telmo
Buenos Aires, Argentina

Mercato Metropolitano
London, UK

The Milk Market
Limerick, Ireland

Khlong Toei Market
Bangkok, Thailand

Torvehallerne
Copenhagen, Denmark

Nadi Market
Nadi, Fiji

Khari Baoli Market
Deli, India

Bodrum Farmers Market
Bodrum, Turkey

The Galway Market,
Galway, Ireland

Östermalm Indoor Market
Stockholm, Sweden

Killavullen Farmers' Market
Cork, Ireland

CREATING A SACRED EATING SPACE

We tend to spend a significant amount of time focusing on what we eat, with the environment in which we eat often getting ignored. One of the most important healthy eating habits we can create is to set up a sacred space and eating environment to positively influence how well we receive our food.

Kitchen tables and worksurfaces can often be a catch-all for leftovers, empty glasses, homework, keys, computers, mobile phones and toys. Can you relate to this? Sitting and eating in that type of environment can affect how we consume food. We are likely to eat more quickly with less joy and pleasure.

Nourishing your body can be one of the most pleasing, satisfying, health-promoting and enjoyable experiences but if you're eating environment is noisy, cluttered and distracting then much of that nourishment becomes lost. Food is not the only thing we need to consider. It is also how we accept, acknowledge and receive our food that can take our nutrition potential to a different level. Creating a sacred eating space brings new energy, purpose, intention and love to the eating experience. When you eat in a nice table setting, you become more relaxed, grateful, aware and connected to the nourishment you receive from your food.

Eating is not merely a physical act. There is an incredible spiritual component to food and when we tap into that we receive the most from this nutrition. You can create a sacred table and form new habits to optimise your eating experience by:

- Getting a new tablecloth to add new energy and colour
- Setting the table as if you were inviting guests over
- Lighting some candles to help create a warm and comforting environment
- Playing music in the background that invites calm and relaxation
- Buying some fresh flowers weekly or keeping a plant on your table to add colour and vibrancy
- Making your table a mobile free zone

A lot of the time we can all fail to connect with our food. Creating a sacred space invites us to be present and provides essential moments to nourish, replenish and receive our food to the fullest.

FOOD STAPLES ALL YEAR ROUND

Cheese

An ideal source of healthy fats, protein, calcium and rich in Vitamins A and B12 that work to support heart health, brain function and gut health. With so many varieties it has become an extremely versatile ingredient in the world of food.

Cabbage

This plant-based leafy green vegetable packed with Vitamins C and K can help aid the body from a vast amount of health conditions such as heart disease and diabetes.

Mushrooms

This leafy green vegetable offers a variety of Vitamins A, C, E, K and minerals as well as fibre and antioxidants making it beneficial for the thyroid function, heart health and bone health.

Potatoes

Grown as an annual vegetable crop, with around 5,000 varieties available worldwide, they are a great source of Vitamins B1, B3, B6 and minerals all year round. What differentiates them is their texture and the vast range of ways they can be cooked.

FOOD STAPLES ALL YEAR ROUND

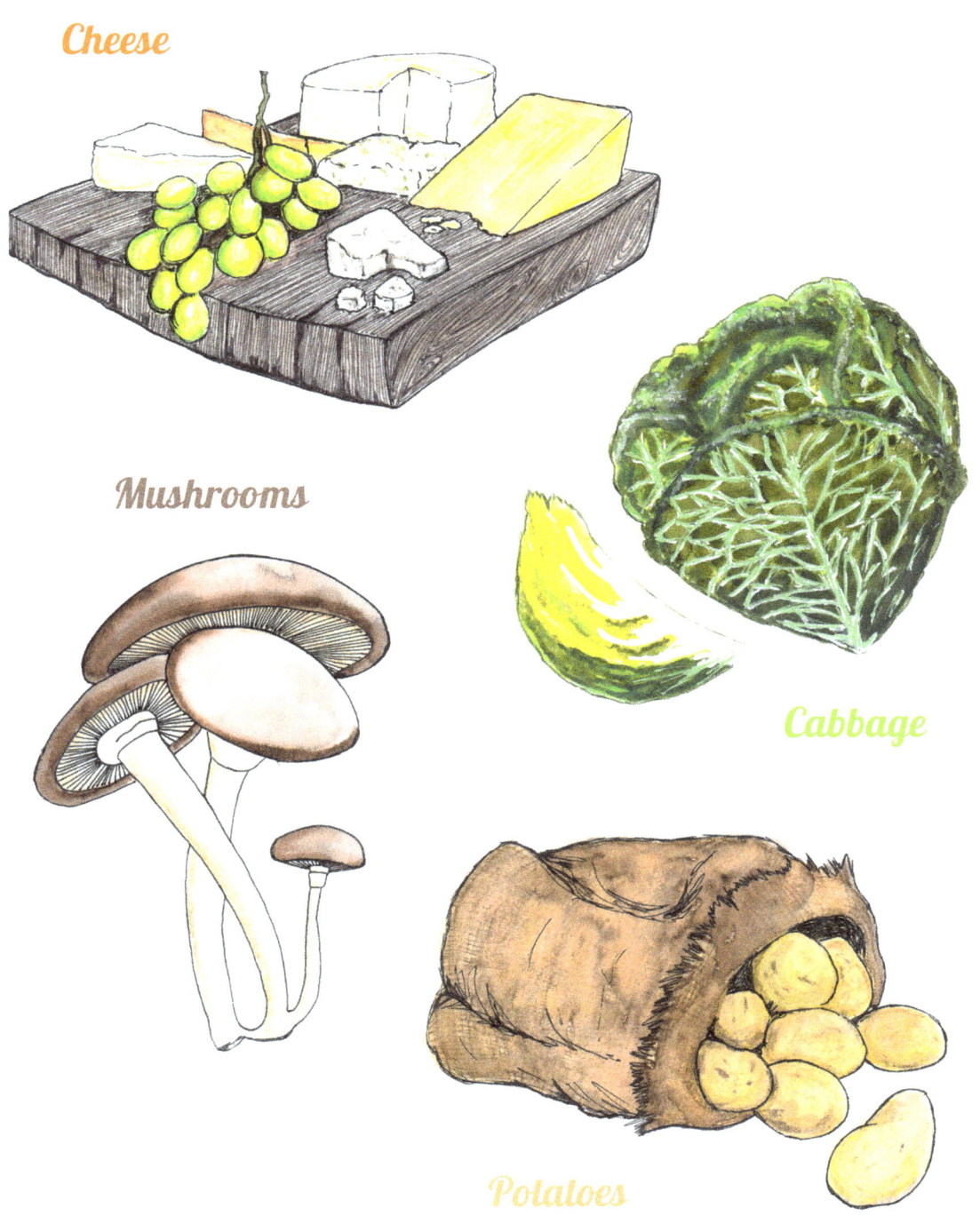

Cheese

Mushrooms

Cabbage

Potatoes

TOP TIPS

Clean out your fridge and food presses
It can be extremely satisfying to have a good clean kitchen. Organise everything using glass jars and air-tight sealed containers. Decluttering your kitchen space will also help declutter your mind, giving you a clearer focus.

Become mindful of the food you put into your body
The food we nourish our body with allows us to fuel our daily lifestyles. Try to eat as much natural, fresh and as many unprocessed foods as possible and drink plenty of water. Making gradual adjustments to your daily food consumption will help make a big difference to your health both now and in the future.

Explore the great outdoors and connect with nature
This is a great informal natural awareness practice. We often get busy, and our mind can begin to race ahead of us. Take stock of your local environment and develop an appreciation of all the food sources that can be sourced from reputable food producers.

Stop self-judgement
Be compassionate towards yourself. Give yourself a break and at times find a quiet space to help your thoughts.

EPILOGUE

Years tend to pass by quickly and with that each of the seasons come and go. That's the ebb and flow beauty of nature's life cycle.

Taking the time to practice mindful eating and gratitude is extremely important. When we make the effort, we begin to realise how much it can impact our lives on both a personal level as well as the wider community level in which we live in. The practice of mindful eating takes patience and understanding to cultivate, but the rewards reaped from taking the time to incorporate it into our daily lives is immense. It enables us to become more aware of and appreciate each of the seasons and the natural world around us. This brings with it a new foundation and baseline from which we can centre awareness on food consumption, and the impact it has on both our environment and our own mental and physical wellbeing.

Well done for taking the time to self-reflect, discover, understand, accept and work on your own self-love development, depending on the season that you started using this journal. This type of listening, healing and learning from your own personal space is extremely important. Like the different change in each of the seasons, food can find ways into our lives to help us grow, evolve and adapt to our ever-changing needs. There are no synchronicities between us and in all that it provides. We need to listen and learn from nature and it in turn will fulfil us in many ways.

"The soil that you walk upon
The soil you treat as dirt
Is the magical material that turns into leaf, flower and fruit." - Isha Sadhguru

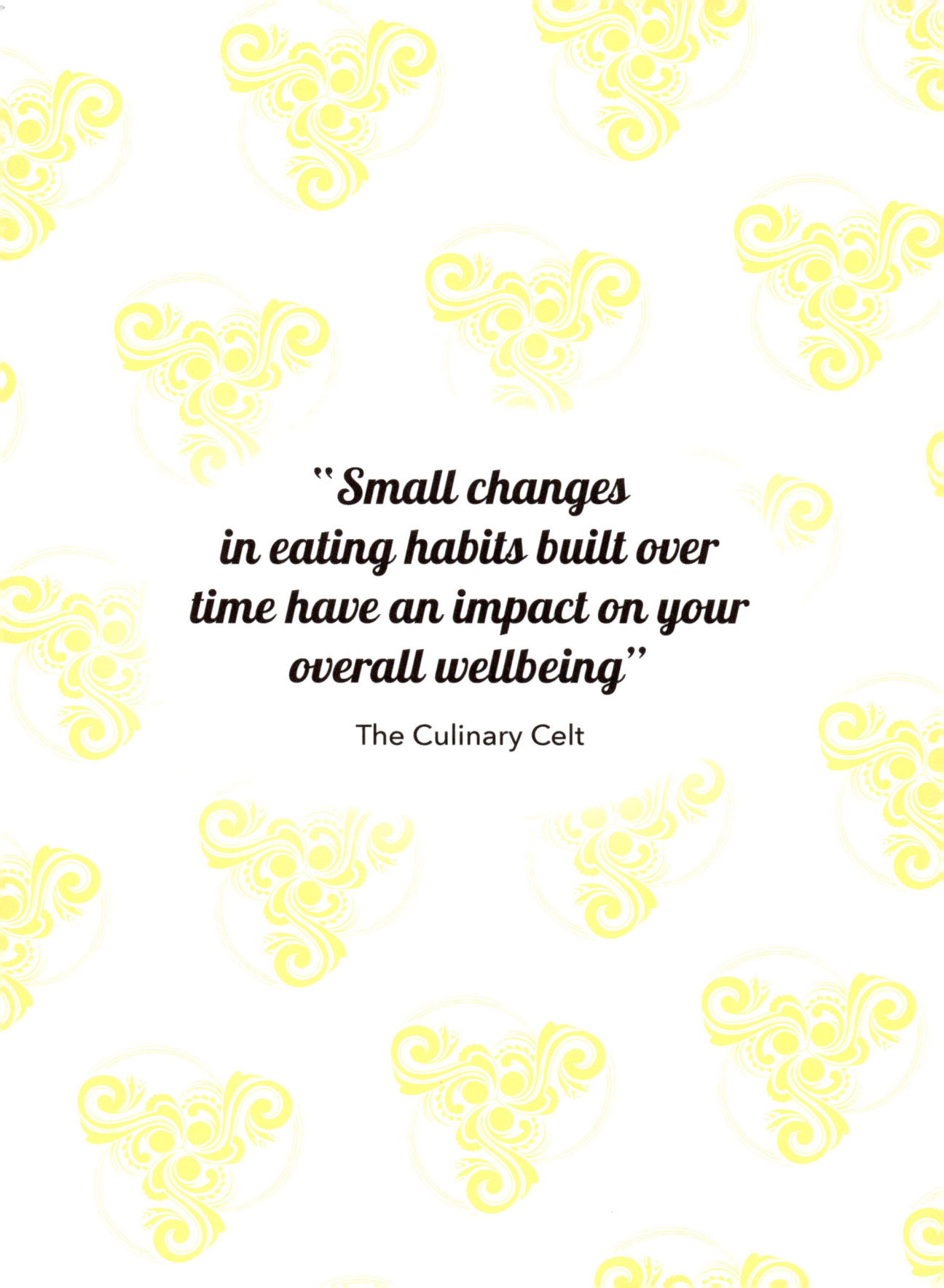

"Small changes in eating habits built over time have an impact on your overall wellbeing"

The Culinary Celt

NOTES

NOTES

NOTES

NOTES

NOTES

> *"Enjoy and explore the foods in your region"*
>
> The Culinary Celt

ABOUT THE AUTHOR

Cathy Fitzgibbon (aka The Culinary Celt) is from County Cork, Ireland. Cathy is a media sales and marketing professional for the past 22 years. She is passionate about exploring contemporary culinary experiences and actively promotes the areas of food sustainably and wellbeing through her food writing contributions and marketing activities, using an ethically based farm to fork ethos. Through her own personal experiences over the past three decades, Cathy has nurtured seasonal eating patterns and thoughtfulness into her daily relationship with food and her natural environment. This practice has helped her inspire, educate and ignite others to develop their own ways to enjoy food in more practical and sustainable ways.

You can learn more about Cathy on
www.theculinarycelt.com
and via her social media platforms -
@theculinarycelt

"We must become the change we want to see"

Mahatma Gandhi

www.ingramcontent.com/pod-product-compliance
Lightning Source LLC
LaVergne TN
LVHW072017060526
838200LV00060B/4694